THE RESOURCE FOR
SMALL GROUP WORSHIP
LEADER'S MANUAL

THE RESOURCE FOR SMALL GROUP WORSHIP LEADER'S MANUAL

CHRIS BOWATER

First published in 2000 by
KEVIN MAYHEW LTD
Buxhall
Stowmarket
Suffolk IP14 3BW

© 2000 Chris Bowater

ISBN 184003 509 9
Catalogue No. 1450169

Cover design by Jonathan Stroulger
Edited by Helen Elliot
Project Co-ordinator: Asher Gregory

Printed in Great Britain

Contents

Introduction

There's no place like home

It is almost impossible to express definitively what worship is. Certainly it is more than the interminable singing of songs that typifies so much of our corporate worship times. Sadly, worship has become almost solely a musical activity, when in fact it is so much more. Worship must always be a vibrant, multi-dynamic expression of adoration, awe and thankfulness. The Creator of all things deserves more than 'a song or two', a medley of thematically linked songs! In reality, worship is not intended to enrich God; telling him for example, that he is great cannot make him greater; but it can enrich us!

So often, when it comes to small group worship, the tendency is to reproduce large, celebration-style gatherings. The intensity of time and passion that the large celebration justifiably generates is almost impossible to produce or sustain in the small church or cell group setting. All too easily the people become discouraged as the not-too-proficient guitarist grinds the worship into the carpet. The group becomes lost in wonder, love and exhaustion! They then move from being willing participators to becoming embarrassed spectators. 'Spectatorism' is the antithesis of true praise and worship. Remember, you are in a home or at least with a body of like-minded individuals which the Bible calls 'the family of God'. You're not in the Albert Hall or the Big Top at a Spring Harvest celebration. Let this be a place where the members can feel 'at home', be natural, be themselves. Perhaps 'normal church' life does not encourage that dynamic. Is it possible that the Church has become more concerned with putting on an event, a programme, rather than loving people, releasing them into their full potential, and giving everyone a genuine sense of value and worth. More interested in the game plan than the players on the field? Groups offer a marvellous opportunity to discover the rich contributions that can come from the people. Often, the very close proximity of other people's lives deepens our knowledge and understanding of God and his ways as they are allowed to express their preferences, feelings and expectations. In seeing the best and worst in each other, God's grace has an opportunity to be operative in our lives. We learn together the ways of forgiveness, patience, thankfulness and mercy.

Love becomes an action

This is not 'going to church', this is 'being' the church. There is something very intimate and real about worship with and in front of a small group of people whom we have come to know and trust. We are gently led into checking out the authenticity of the heart, words and actions. There's no hiding place. These are people we know and care about. This produces reality. Careful maintenance of superficial relationships produces a group of strangers. There is good cognitive Bible study and ministry but we can still cover up our weaknesses and our real lives. We share about safe things rather than real things. Koinonia – intimate fellowship amongst Christians – seldom just happens. It takes time and hard work. It takes people who want to do the nitty-gritty work of developing a community of Christian friends.

It takes more than a cup of tea to make someone feel welcome, though it helps. The atmosphere of the home, the disposition of the leader and the other members are crucial to helping the reserved and the reluctant to relax. A suitable CD playing goes a long way to covering embarrassed silence. Family photo albums always encourage natural conversations and young children, post-bathtime and pre-bedtime, always seem to bring life and lightness into the room since they haven't yet learned to be religious! Perhaps we are too pre-occupied with starting a meeting when in reality the greatest challenge is simply to get people to meet.

As we understand that our corporate worship experience is more than singing songs, we will discover that everything we do can be meaningful worship. Let the time together be filled with encouragement as well as exhortation. Leadership style is of great significance here. Determine that, as well as information given, there will be opportunities for personal insights to be shared. This is when proceedings can grind to an embarrassingly silent halt. It may come as a surprise, but many who attend our churches are neither used to or expecting to be involved. A deep lack of self-worth can lurk behind even the most gregarious mask. Everyone wants to be wanted and to have a sense of belonging. Those who feel worthless amongst fellow Christians will also carry a strong sense of non-acceptance when it comes to God. Human and spiritual affirmation takes time and care. We must teach by word and example the value God places on each of us. This is foundational to a release of worship that is real and meaningful.

1 A Heart for Worship

As the deer pants for streams of water,
so my soul pants for you, O God.
My soul thirsts for God, for the living God.
When can I go and meet with God?

Psalm 42:1,2

The Desire for God A desire to know God, to meet with him. This is the key to the Spirit-filled worship of God. Without this desire to stand in his presence, worship becomes a pointless experience. Worship that is without expectation, without a tangible sense of the presence of God, is fruitless.

As we worship God in Spirit and reality we receive from God. However, our motivation must always be that we worship him for who he is. Worship is for God. It is not in order to fulfil some self-centred desire, to make us feel good, or to obtain any other kind of benefit or blessing. Thirst for the Giver of Living Water more than the experience of refreshing. Worship is for God simply because he is worth it! He's worth it all! None the less, because God is obedient and faithful to his own word – 'it's better to give than to receive' – because it is impossible to 'out give' God, the One who inhabits the praises of his people, or dwells and reigns in the environment of praise – he loves to be generous with his children. He presences himself with us, not as a spectator but as a giver of gifts. We ask for mercy, he gives grace to help in our times of need. He gives us his peace. In his presence we experience the gift of full joy.

We worship too because we have been called to worship. We've been called and chosen to be a 'kingdom of priests'. This is man's highest calling. Not to be obsessed with activity and self interest. It is not doing but being. We are to live as those who reign and rule in life, carrying the fragrance of the priestly anointing. Saturated in the oil of the Spirit, we are to be those who are 'set aside for his Glory'.

The Presence of God

God is always present. By the very nature of being eternal, he is omnipresent.

The eyes of the Lord are everywhere,
keeping watch on the wicked and the good.

Proverbs 15:3

Where can I go from your Spirit?
Where can I flee from your presence?
If I go up to the heavens, you are there;
if I make my bed in the depths, you are there.

Psalm 139:7, 8

How much of my life is lived in the constant awareness of God's nearness and presence? The God who is everywhere wants to reveal himself somewhere.

- For Moses the somewhere was a burning bush. A wilderness encounter that turned a prince into a liberator.

- For Jacob the somewhere was a wrestling match. A man on-the-run discovered that God could run faster.

- For Saul the somewhere was a pre-conversion flash of light, an audible voice, that led to a change of name and a change of heart.

The God who is everywhere delights to reveal and manifest his presence. He loves to meet with his people and especially revels in the environment of praise.

But thou art holy,
O thou that inhabitest the praises of Israel.

Psalm 22:3 (KJB)

Thou who art enthroned upon the praises of Israel.

Psalm 22:3 (NAS)

Sometimes in scripture the manifested presence of God is referred to as his 'glory'.

The trumpeters and singers joined in unison,
as with one voice, to give praise and thanks to the Lord.
Accompanied by trumpets, cymbals and other instruments,
they raised their voices in praise to the Lord and sang:
'He is good; his love endures for ever.'
Then the temple of the Lord was filled with a cloud,
and the priests could not perform their services
because of the cloud,
for the glory of the Lord filled the temple of God.

2 Chronicles 5:13, 14

When the priests withdrew from the Holy Place,
the cloud filled the temple of the Lord.
And the priests could not perform their service
because of the cloud,
for the glory of the Lord filled his temple.
Then Solomon said,
'The Lord has said that he would dwell in a dark cloud;
I have indeed built a magnificent temple for you,
a place for you to dwell for ever.'

1 Kings 8:10-13

Imagine the awesome reality of God's presence. God in the house! How tangible and real. Without his presence the gathering is bland and predictable. Without the recognition, acknowledgement and affirmation of his presence the gathering is a mere 'act' of worship, a futile formula and, at best, a superficial religious indulgence.

Immanence and Eminence

Most people acknowledge the greatness, vastness, power and majesty of God, and can readily sing the

13

great hymns of heritage and faith:

Immortal, invisible,
God only wise;
in light inaccessible
hid from our eyes.

Walter Chalmers Smith

Jesus! The name high over all,
in hell, or earth, or sky;
angels and mortals prostrate fall
and devils fear and fly.

Charles Wesley

or, more recently

Lord of Lords, King of Kings,
Maker of heaven and earth and all good things.

Jessy Dixon, Randy Scruggs, John Thompson

We worship him for his unsurpassed greatness. If we are not careful, we make him out to be the God who watches' us 'from a distance', instead of opening our eyes to the One who is near, here, moving by his Spirit. Sadly, even the songs we sometimes sing imply that God has to be persuaded to leave whatever he is doing, to be convinced that our meeting is worth attending. 'Come! Come!' we cry, only to hear the gentle whisper 'I am here!' He invites us to enter in, into where he is, into what he is doing, listening to what he is saying and perhaps even singing the songs that he is singing!

Jack Hayford says: 'The Scriptures show that God manifested his glory in a visible sense when his order of worship was established and honoured amongst his people.'

His order involves:

- unity of life and vision
- cleanness of hearts and lives
- a profound sense of gratitude and thankfulness.

It is written of Mary and Joseph that:

Thinking that he (Jesus) was in their company, they travelled on for a day.

Luke 2:44

It is worth wondering how many days, weeks, months or even years, have been 'travelled' by individuals and churches who assumed the Lord's presence. Large congregations, fine preaching, accomplished musicians or even successful meetings do not constitute or guarantee his presence. It is not a matter of style, traditional or radical. It is the positioning of the heart of people that causes God to respond. We may spend much of our energies on cosmetic presentation. God looks upon the heart. We can rearrange the furniture of worship: informality replacing liturgy; the latest worship resource in place of traditional hymns; the hymn book itself can be sidelined in favour of the overhead projector, or to be really up-to-date, computer-generated images and words. God still cries:

Rend your hearts and not your garments.

Joel 2:13

There is often so much preoccupation with external matters that the real issues are ignored. There will always be more 'things' that would assist the programme and presentation: more efficient PA; better quality musical instruments, to name but the obvious.

In the valid pursuit of clearer communication, seeker-friendly ambience, cultural relevance and general upgrading and updating, let us not lose sight of this single priority: we need to see and experience more of the life-imparting presence of God. And then, when by his grace that happens, we need to avoid becoming complacent or satisfied, and to hunger and thirst for even more!

David, the Psalmist, was a man possessed by a passion for the glory of God. His great heart for God and his presence was David's greatest strength. He excelled at many things:

- serving his father
- looking after the sheep
- music and poetry
- warrior skills
- leadership and kingliness.

His dependency on and relationship with God was the reason for his success. His demise was directly linked to a season of self-reliance and independence.

I have set the Lord always before me.
Because he is at my right hand,
I shall not be shaken.

Psalm 16:8

David had a heart for God. His passion for God was the mainspring, the driving force and the love of his life. He loved God for himself, not just for what he did for him. He had tasted of the Lord's goodness. He had first-hand experience of God. His relationship with God began in the solitude of the hills and fields. He would write and sing his songs, not because it was his ministry responsibility but simply as an offering of devotion. A public profile and platform was not the motivation for his worship. He loved God. God was real to him; as real as life, breath, creation, even as real as the very sheep for which he cared. He delighted himself in the Lord and he desperately wanted to know God more. His chief desire was:

To gaze upon the beauty of the Lord.

Psalm 27:4

The deepest cry of his heart was:

Do not cast me from your presence
or take your Holy Spirit from me.

Psalm 51:11

The Evidence Surely a fair definition of having a meeting is to actually meet with someone. Whenever Christian fellowship becomes too 'religious', usually the first thing to suffer is genuine life sharing, friendship and interaction. This applies to both our human and spiritual needs for relationship. Never lose the desire to encounter the living, life-changing God.

Let us look at what we can call 'the evidence' of God's presence:

1 *It is possible!*

God really wants to be with his people, in the environment of love and praise. It is his natural habitat. The presence of the Holy Spirit reveals the heart and nature of God to us. He brings a deeper appreciation and understanding of the Father. He always draws us closer to Jesus. It is what he does!

2 *It is promised!*

God never wants to leave us on our own, leave us to our own resources. Neither does he want to be a spectator at his own service! He wants to be welcomed. That does not mean he has to be persuaded, cajoled or convinced. He is present. But the manifestation of his presence . . . ?

3 *It is provisional!*

There are conditions. God looks for those who desire to live:

- in oneness with fellow believers
- in obedience to his Word
- in openness and thankfulness.

Oneness Unity does not mean uniformity. The Church is not a cult. God demonstrated his love of variety in the earth and the universe, he celebrates diversity in the expression of his heart through the individual. The Church is a corporate entity where people are not cloned, everyone looking and sounding like each other. In the same way, the Creator's expression of Christ is revealed through individuals who reflect his love. Individualism is not acceptable, while the individual is valued. Individuals need each other, it is called 'fellowship'.

The word 'fellowship' comes from the Greek word, *koinonia*, and means 'communion, sharing in common, joint participation'. It was the word used to describe the marriage relationship and business partnership. Fellowship is a sharing or togetherness based on mutual trust and commitment. Think of it in these terms – 'fellows on a ship'.

The Apostle Paul wrote:

I thank my God upon every remembrance of you, always in every prayer of mine for you all making request with joy, for your fellowship in the gospel from the first day until now; being confident of this very thing, that he which hath begun a good work in you will perform it until the day of Jesus Christ.

Philippians 1:3-6 (NAS)

They continued steadfastly in . . . fellowship.

Acts 2:42 (NAS)

Fellowship may be a fairly dated concept, but perhaps expressing it as working at and maintaining relationships is more easily understood. Relationships involve:

1 The family of God

God, in his Word, calls his Church a family, and when we are born into it, we automatically acquire many brothers and sisters. Then follows a life of involvement and interaction. In the family atmosphere we grow and mature, our lives are shaped, and we are transformed into the image of Christ in an experiential way. Every child of God needs a strong, secure home in which to grow. It is tragic when spiritual children abandon their spiritual family and go out and attempt to raise themselves. This is both unhealthy and dangerous. Imbalance invariably results, and because proper discipline is lacking, confusion and despair often take hold. Fellowship is participating in the life of a home, harmonising and co-operating with the family that God has placed you with.

Read also: Matthew 12:46-50; Luke 8:19-21; Psalm 68:6.

2 Walking in love

In Isaiah Chapter 2 a tremendous prophetic word is given. It is an invitation to the 'Mountain of the Lord'. Isaiah was speaking beyond his day to a day when a spiritual gathering would occur out of all nations of the earth, a gathering that would have as its focus the presence of God and the House of the Lord. This word takes in the entire new covenant day (the time between the first and second coming of Christ). God draws us, God teaches us, but within that he also requires something of us, and that which he requires is the transformation of our swords into ploughshares and our spears into pruning hooks.

Nation shall not lift up sword against nation,
neither shall they learn war any more.

Isaiah 2:4 (NRSV)

The edifying, building up, of one another replaces the destructive, tearing down spirit of the unloving world from which we came. A call goes out to the people of God (here called the House of Jacob):

Come ye, and let us walk in the light of the Lord.

Isaiah 2:5

Read also: 1 John 2:10-11; 1 Corinthians 1:9-10; John 13:35.

3 Principle of forgiveness

Wherever true biblical fellowship relationships exist among a people of God, there the spirit of forgiveness must of necessity also exist. Forgiveness will carry us through times of interpersonal conflict, disagreement and offence. Each of us has certain personality traits, strengths and weaknesses, idiosyncrasies, and quirks that can irritate others, and beyond that we also make mistakes.

We all stumble in many ways.

James 3:2

These mistakes, omissions and sins can offend and injure, and further, they have the potential to damage relationships. If the love and forgiveness of Christ is not operating in us, when we face strain in relationships, our reaction will be to sever the relationship. This reaction, one that reveals the natural heart of man, is diametrically opposed to the nature of Jesus and the life of the Holy Spirit within. God's way is forgiveness. God's way is reconciliation. One of the most important, far-reaching and personally rewarding principles that we will ever be called upon to learn is that of forgiveness in the House of the Lord.

Read also: Matthew 18:19-35; Matthew 6:12, 14-15; Ephesians 4:32; Colossians 3:13; Galatians 6:1.

Obedience Though God is always present, the manifestation of that presence, God revealing himself in the context of worship, is conditional. There is usually a stated or implied 'if' when it comes to knowing his presence: 'When two or three, if gathered together in my Name . . . I will be in the midst.' The 'if' implies obedience to God's Word, his purposes and his ways. Submission to God releases spiritual power and authority.

Submit yourselves then to God.
Resist the devil, and he will flee from you.

James 4:7

- His Word, a lamp to our feet and a light to our path, releases guidance.
- In all your ways acknowledge him, releases direction.
- Seek first the Kingdom of God and his righteousness releases provision.

Worship is a place where we learn obedience and submission: to God and to each other. In loving God we learn to love one another. As we discover the wonders of God in each other, we learn to trust him more for ourselves.

Openness and Thankfulness

Worship is the place of gratitude. Worship is a lifestyle of thanksgiving. In our openness to bring to God the

21

requests of our hearts and lives he teaches us to blend our requests with thanksgiving. Thanksgiving is at the heart of worship. Learning in all things to say 'thank you', regardless of the circumstances. Worship is not conditioned by our circumstances but our worship will affect our circumstances.

Read Psalm 63. Here the Psalmist is in a desert. Literal or spiritual? Whichever, it caused him to be desperate, tired and very thirsty.

- He knew his God: 'You are my God.'

- He knew where to look: 'I seek you earnestly.'

- He meant it: 'My soul longs for you.'

- He knew his condition: 'In a dry and weary land where there is no water.'

- He gives thanks for better times: 'I have seen you in the sanctuary.'

The choices we make in times of distress, trouble and hardship determine a pattern for our lives. Here, David makes a great choice: 'My lips will praise you.' He has remembered the works and the ways of his God. He has 'seen the Lord'. No one and nothing can take this away from him. Instead of bringing the sand of his dry experience into the sanctuary, he brings the sanctuary into the desert. Even the sand of the desert becomes holy ground. Discovering the presence of God in the midst of his suffering, he declares: 'Under the shadow of your wings I will sing.' This is worship in the midst of life's challenges. This is thankfulness in the face of hardship.

This came from a man who had a heart for worship.

2 Created to be Creative

With my whole heart, I will bless you.
With my whole life, I will honour you,
and with all that I have, and am and long to be
I'll worship you, worship you . . .
So make my whole life as living worship,
worship unto you.

Chris Bowater, Sovereign Lifestyle 1986

In His Image Made in God's image and after his likeness (Genesis 1:26) we have the potential for creativity directly inherited from Father God, Creator of all things, visible and invisible, all substance and thought. Because creativity is inherent in us, there is a deep-rooted longing or desire to create, to change the environment, to invent and develop ideas. We want to 'take after Father'.

The brain controls mind and body, different areas of the brain being responsible for intellect, dominance, speech, vision; there is a centre for music, better developed in some brains than others; a centre for interpreting on paper what the eye sees; a centre controlling body movements. Each person has the potential to be creative, with built-in basic essentials, but as a garden is made up of a variety of flowers, basically the same but vastly different in colour, size, design, scent, leaf, so it is with the creative ability of God's people.

Our creativity reflects our attitude towards God, not by the skill or quality of the product, but in the desire to create. We were made 'for the praise of his glory'. We can only offer back to God what he has bestowed upon us, with thanksgiving and in worship. It is our responsible service, for him to use for his purposes – to bless, to heal, to teach, to reveal himself, to give pleasure and joy.

Defining Creativity The dictionary states that 'to create' means 'to make something from nothing'. By this definition, only God can be truly creative. Man can only use what God has placed at his disposal, making 'something out of something'. We are, at best, only second-hand creators.

1 *To create . . . for what purpose?*

- For the purpose of God's glory.

- For the blessing of others.

- For personal pleasure and benefit to self.

2 *To be, or not to be . . . creative*

We were created to be creative. How we use our creativity is up to each individual. Some people appear to have more than a fair share of creative ability, but many do not recognise their activities as acceptable creative praise. Some do not believe in their own abilities, and some place too much emphasis on the recognition of others. If creativity is directed heaven-ward, there are no boundaries, no rights or wrongs; the only limits being our own skills, materials available, and ideas of how they can be used in praise, with a heart sincere in its desire to worship God. We are not creating an object to be worshipped, nor are we trying to impress God, or use our creativity for self-indulgence. Creative praise can be expressed:

- Physically, through dance, drama, interpretative movement; in the use of sign language, with streamers, flags, even clapping and waving arms.

- In music, the most widely accepted expression in the Church, with the use of instruments, vocals, in song writing and the spontaneous 'song of the Lord'.

- Through the visual arts, employed as a means of praise in the Church for centuries; paintings, murals, collage, banners, architecture and design; also sculpture, carving, embroidery, weaving, ceramics, metal-work, stained glass

CREATED TO BE CREATIVE

and of course, flower arranging. Photography is now entering the scene. We have used transparencies with music and narration to interpret psalms, or creation, as an avenue to praise.

• Meals, table-settings, communication and friendship, sharing God's love in many different ways, can be counted in the never-ending list of creativity, and therefore, praise.

3 Creative praise is historical and traditional

Skilled craftsmen have been employed by the Church to create environments for worship for centuries. They worked in stone, wood, metal; designing magnificent stained glass windows, sewing rich vestments and embroidering stoles, furnishings, and wall hangings. They made candlesticks, chalices, screens and decorated manuscripts using intricate artwork and calligraphy. They used colours to represent seasons of the Church calendar, purple, green, white or gold, red, related to mood and emotion. Music, singing, chanting, processions, pageantry and drama were all vitally important in days when people were mostly illiterate.

Symbolism and its use in the Church make an interesting study. 'Logos' or simple pictures, representing words or ideas, were used as visual aids for praise. Today banners used in worship often carry symbols such as the fish, the Chi Rho, the cross and the dove, a sort of 'shorthand' for the expression of great truths. These are sometimes called 'ChrisMons' (Christian Monograms).

4 Creativity starts with God

The Old Testament is bursting with God's ideas for the use of materials, colour and design. After the first great act of creation, we find God in the construction business, designing a practical house-boat-cum-floating zoo (Genesis 6). He gives instructions for the tabernacle, a temporary place of worship (Exodus 35) and designs for the colourful priestly garments, even the order of precious stones on the high priest's breast-piece (Exodus 29, 39). In Exodus 37, God gives instructions for the ark of covenant, and in 2 Chronicles 3, Solomon builds the temple according to the word of the Lord delivered to David in 1 Chronicles 28. The second temple is revealed to Ezekiel in a vision (Ezekiel 40) complete with carvings and ornaments. Celebrations, songs and victory processions with music are ordered by God (Ezra 3; Nehemiah 12; Joshua 6; Psalms), part of the temple life.

5 *Built-in creativity*

Four major ingredients are required for creative praise:

- imagination
- sensitivity and knowledge
- natural skills
- spiritual gifting.

Imagination is 'seeing with the mind's eye'. Walking along the beach, I notice a piece of twisted, dirty driftwood. It looks dead, useless, but in my imagination I see a kneeling figure, with outstretched arms. I take it home, to clean, to scrape and sandpaper the wood, until the dirt and roughness are removed, revealing the grain, and red-brown hue; the kneeling figure takes shape. It's like me, I realise! Sometimes I feel like that piece of driftwood – ugly, useless, forgotten. Jesus picks me up, sees the potential in me, and works on me, lovingly, carefully and skilfully, until I become the person he intends me to be, kneeling, worshipping, reaching out to him.

Creative praise is rooted in our imagination.

Sensitivity and knowledge involve and include the understanding of materials, tools, and theory; of how creativity can be used effectively; and the effect of some aspects such as colour, texture, sound, posture, design on mind, body and emotion. They can be used for blessing or have adverse effects. Knowledgeable craftsmanship enhances the quality of creative praise.

Natural skill or ability may be passed on from one generation to another. Co-ordination between mind, eye, hand or body, for precision, or rhythm, or perception is often an inherited, rather than an acquired skill. Creative praise may run in the family (1 Chronicles 25:6, 7).

Spiritual gifting is an added dimension. It changes a natural or inherited talent into something special. The song writer, dancer, photographer may be skilled in a chosen profession, but the Holy Spirit combines talent with inspiration for God's glory.

Creating an Environment for Worship

God uses all aspects of his creation to develop in his people an attitude of praise, and to reveal his presence. He uses buildings, nature, colour, music, movement, garments and craftsmanship. An environment for worship is based on God's example, the designer seeking to meet God's criteria, aiming at creative excellence, using everything at his disposal, aware of how worshippers may be affected by the sensory aspects of their surroundings.

The design of a roof or ceiling may not only relate to acoustics, but may uplift or subdue the spirit. Carpet or bare stone floor, pews or cushioned seats, plain curtains, stained glass windows, banners, candles, flowers, lighting, music and colour tones can affect relationships, behaviour. They can develop the atmosphere of peace, the comfort of home, or promote disruption, or coldness.

Creative praise is a command, a response. It is environmental. It is a joy, a need, a longing of the heart.

3 Maintaining Worship Values

It is essential to understand that even though the format and content of a small group worship experience is very different from that experienced by a larger church congregation or celebration, the worship values which form the foundations of both need not and arguably, must not, change. Indeed, whilst encouraging a different approach to worship in the small group environment, it is essential to realise that disappointment is often experienced solely because of an abandoning of tried and tested values.

What are values? Values form the philosophy, our way of thinking about worship. Influenced by a vast array of life's experiences, education, upbringing, values remain unseen, though they become the guiding factors of all that we think and therefore, invariably, all that we do.

It is crucial to remain true to teaching and revelation, whilst realising there is more to worship than that experienced in larger groups. Here are four suggested values for worship:

- Worship is for God

- Worship is to do with relationships

- Worship is responsive

- Worship is controlled by the Holy Spirit

Discuss them, add to them but establish for yourself a good foundation from which you can build. Use the outline below to stimulate a discussion on the worship values held by your church or small group. There is something very wonderful about a group who not only know their agreed values but own and live them.

1 *Worship is for God*

It's not about a place . . .

It's not about a style . . .

It's not about a preference . . .

It's not about my feelings . . .

It's not about music . . .

Matt Redman wrote:

I'm coming back to the heart of worship . . .
It's all about you, all about you, Jesus.

From the very outset let it be known, 'We're here for the Lord.'

Read: Deuteronomy 5:6-10; Romans 1:20-23.

2 *Worship is to do with relationships*

Relationships with God and with each other. There are both vertical and horizontal implications. I do not exist as an island in my worship with God. Personal relationships are in focus as soon as I say that I love God. I cannot love Him if I am:

living in jealousy

living in bitterness

living in unforgiveness.

My relationship with God needs also to be one that develops through these stages:

nursed child – Isaiah 49:15-16; 1 Peter 2:2

responsible son – Ephesians 4:13; Hebrews 5:14

mature man – Philippians 1:20-23.

3 Worship is responsive

The Bible is full of responsive behaviour that is acceptable to God in worship. We can be free in our gatherings, free in ourselves to express ourselves within the whole spectrum of responses. God needs to touch our narrow thinking, our fears and our culture. Consider:

lifting of hands

singing

shouting

kneeling

bowing

weeping

laughing

standing

falling

. . . and more.

Read the Psalms!

In heaven, the elders worshipped falling on their faces (Revelation 7:11).

4 Worship is controlled by the Holy Spirit

As we learn to trust God and each other, we must learn to trust the work and the activities of the Comforter, the Holy Spirit, and allow our worship be led by him – not by tradition or even by the expectations of others. Certainly not by preference or style.

Do not quench the Holy Spirit.

1 Thessalonians 5:19 (NAS)

4   Small Groups and Relationships

Whenever people start to get close to each other, they invariably begin to scratch each other with their sharp edges. What began as an ideal, a vision for ministry, care and growth, becomes an ordeal as you cope with the reality: that people have different preferences, habits, feelings, expectations, and personalities. You get to see the worst and best in others, and they see it all in you. In a large church you can hide. In small group communities, there are no hiding places. This stage is not to be avoided, but embraced if you want to develop true fellowship.

There is something very intimate and real about worshipping with and in front of a small group whom you have come to know and trust. You are forced to check the authenticity of your heart and your words, because they know you. We sing:

You are Lord, you are Lord.
You have risen from the dead
and you are Lord;
every knee shall bow,
every tongue confess,
that Jesus Christ is Lord.

The Koinonia Community

And because we know each other, we know that these words are worked out in reality in this place.

One of the great benefits of intentionally taking the time, and having the courage, to be part of a small group, is that you get to worship with people whom you know and care about. Some people will say, 'None of this sounds like my small group.' They say this because so many small groups, cells and churches are careful to maintain superficial relationships. We do good systematic Bible study and good ministry work in our small groups, but we really don't get too far in being open or real with each other. We cover up our weaknesses and faults, and when it's time for prayer requests, we keep deliberately vague about our real lives. We share about safe things rather than real things.

Koinonia – intimate fellowship amongst Christians – seldom just happens. It takes time and hard work. It takes people who want to do the nitty-gritty work of developing a community of Christian friends. At the very least, it takes one person who will go out on a limb with the idea of developing a small group that gets beyond the superficial.

Here's how to turn your small group into a *Koinonia* community.

1 Sharing one's story

The first step towards achieving the goal of Koinonia in the small group is for everyone to get to know each other – to share their histories, to tell their stories. Over several weeks, even months, encourage those attending the group to share something of their journey so far. Even use fun group-building activities as a part of the agenda for the meeting. Allow space and time, even encourage questions and answers. Everyone has a story – not always sensational or full of drama; usually, on the surface, rather normal and mundane. But for each of us the story is what has made us what we are.

When we become Christians, the story becomes one that encounters redemption, grace, forgiveness and mercy. These then become the influencing factors of the journey of our lives, either because we have walked away from it or walked in the light and revelation of it. Our story therefore has power and validity.

As we share our stories it becomes easier and safer to share the more vulnerable parts of our lives. When we know each other's background, we can understand a lot of what makes us the individuals we have become. Without this foundational relationship-building, a group seldom feels free to share openly beyond a superficial level.

2 Affirmation

Something remarkable happens in relationships when a person is listened to and affirmed. What happens to most people is we begin to trust each other; we feel safe enough to share more. To be open and real with another person not only takes courage, it takes trust. This place of affirmation is when we say to each other, 'I like you, and I care about you, and you can trust me. I won't use anything you share with me against you, because I have some needs I'm going to share too.' Intentionally taking the time to affirm one another's strengths and giftedness builds trust in a small group.

3 Sharing needs

We sinners are still dealing with our old nature, our tendency to do the wrong things, to be selfish and full of pride. When people have taken time to share their stories with a group, and we have developed a trust and a bond of confidentiality and care in that group, it is possible to ask each other to share real prayer requests and reveal what really is going on in our hearts.

All of this may feel like a bridge too far, or at least an unrealistic vision. In reality this may be true. But without a vision we die and dead people are no use to anyone. I'd rather fail in the attempt than miss the possibility or opportunity. There has to be something better than our corporate isolationism and individualism. There is something better than being together: it's being *together*, together!

Rules for Relationships

Be eager to maintain the unity of the Spirit in the bond of peace. . . until we attain to the unity of faith and of the knowledge of the Son of God, to mature manhood, to the measure of the stature of the fullness of Christ.

Ephesians 4:3, 13 (RSV)

In Ephesians 4 and 5 Paul compares unity of spirit – right attitude of heart and mind toward one another in spite of weakness or sin – with unity of faith – absolute maturity and doctrinal perfection.

This is the challenge!

Be eager to maintain the unity of the Spirit until we attain the unity of faith.

There are three implications:

1 The unity of the Spirit must be the priority until God brings his Church to the unity of faith.

2 We must show eagerness in desiring to maintain this unity of the Spirit.

3 We cannot and must not insist on the unity of faith, in which relationship, love and care for one another is conditional on spiritual maturity or doctrinal purity. We all see 'in part, as through a darkened glass', and need to accept each other on that basis.

Practical rules for building relationships

1 Maintain an attitude of humility, meekness, patience and forbearance.

Humility is being willing to be known for who we are more than for what we have done. It means we are prepared to do anything necessary to make matters right with others when we have sinned against them, offended or hurt them.

Meekness means not insisting on doing things our way or pushing ourselves forward.

Patience waits for others, with love and consideration, even when they are wrong, for God to make us aware of his timing in their lives.

Forbearance involves being available to others in their struggles and weaknesses, to help, protect, cover and care.

2 We are to speak the truth in love (Ephesians 4:15, 25, 26, 29-31).

Much attention needs to be given to the use of words. The tongue can be as a knife, cursing or blessing. Several things about our speech habits may need to be taken care of. Keeping friendships? Friendships that glorify Christ? These friendships are built on trust and truthfulness and these are relationships that please and honour Christ. How often we are forced into relationships and friendships that never confront truth, right living and integrity in each other. We must value the friend so much that, in Christ's time and in his way, we live in openness and truth.

Speak the truth. Make sure that the relationship is one of being 'in love'. Only where there is love is there a right to speak. The relationship gives that right to one another. It doesn't exist without love. Don't be sentimental, be direct. Do not speak about what is rumour, but only that which you know to be true.

In love. Not in anger or out of bitterness. Do not be unkind but wait for God's timing. He who is Truth knows best when and how to speak. Wait for him to prepare the heart of the friend. Be careful what you speak. Wisdom sometimes remains silent.

Speak that which edifies. Only speak that which is helpful and positive. It is not acceptable to say, 'I was only being honest'. Even honesty can cause devastation. The issue is greater than honesty. Honesty without wisdom can actually be sin.

3 Paul exhorts believers to forgive those who sin and to discipline those who do not repent of their sins (Ephesians 4:32; 5:1, 5-7). There is no problem of disunity

that cannot be solved by greater humility and forgiveness.

4 We must acknowledge that we belong to each other. We are co-heirs of his grace (Ephesians 4:25).

5 Paul exhorts us to:

- be filled with the Holy Spirit

- worship the Lord

- encourage one another

- always and in everything give thanks to God the Father.

How do we make small group relationships work, meaningfully and in a way that honours the Lord? The keys are:

Gratefulness Encouragement Thanksgiving

5 Transition and the Traditional Church

As I travel across the country and from nation to nation leading celebrations, seminars, conferences and concerts, sometimes in the smaller, more traditional churches, it is obvious to me that contemporary worship is still a volatile issue. Part of a congregation is for it; others resist. Sometimes the church becomes polarised into a sort of armed camp – the hymn singers versus the chorus singers.

At the start of a new millennium, it has to be said, it's not as accentuated as it used to be. I remember when the introduction of a guitar was on a par with the naming of anti-Christ. It was perceived to be the beginning of the end of Christian civilisation as we knew it! The addition of drums and all things electronic was greeted by howls of dismay, aggressive annual general meetings on the one hand, and dismissive derision on the other. How things can change in thirty years!

Today, it is more likely that radicals and traditionalists will co-exist, giving each other space to express differing styles of worship. This may be more of a logistical solution than a genuine operation of exercising grace. Am I exaggerating? Recently, I led worship in a church where half the congregation sang when I led a hymn, and the others kept silent. When I led a more contemporary worship song, the hymn lovers kept silent while the chorus lovers sang. The issue here was obviously not worship!

For every church I see working its way successfully through the praise/worship transition, dozens get bogged down in the power struggle over issues:

- How many contemporary songs?

- Vineyard, Maranatha, Hillsong, Kendrick, Bowater, Redman, Smith . . .?

- Should we clap, have drums, a worship team?

- What about the hymns?

But one thing is constantly true, when change is attempted through an emphasis of externals only, the church is unlikely to become a worshipping church. At best it will simply exchange one musical style for another.

More Attitude than Style

It is one thing to help a church change its style of music; it is another thing to help change its attitude. If you are the one with the vision for the church, desiring to move them into vibrant, exuberant praise, it is easy to become frustrated. Keep always in mind that you are wanting to move people beyond the common fund of experience, and only the Holy Spirit can do that. Play contemporary music tapes for them all you like, until there is a change of heart, people will only pay lip service to your ideas.

Change does not occur overnight. It can even take several years, by teaching and mentoring, and most importantly, a sovereign work of the Holy Spirit, first of all in the heart of leaders.

Three Essentials I believe there are three essentials required to lead churches through the praise/worship transition. To leave out any one of these will shortchange the process and produce superficial results.

1 People must be taught the biblical principles which serve as a foundation for praise and worship. They must be led to understand why they do what they do. Without this understanding, there is lack of purpose and a lack of expectancy, both of which demotivate the worshipper.

2 We must provide an opportunity for people to enter into worship experiences that reinforce these principles.

Understanding the concept of entering God's presence is important. Experiencing it in a time of worship is life changing.

3   We must undergird the praise and worship ministry of the church with prayer. People only become worshippers as the Holy Spirit reveals to them the Father's character and his unconditional love and grace. Only then can they rejoice in who they are in Christ. As revelation continues, they become free to express spontaneous celebratory praise.

Praise increases as revelation increases.

Practically speaking, how can these essentials be incorporated into a small church/group?

By teaching

Revelation and understanding come by teaching. Worship is not learned by osmosis. It does not just happen by some Darwinian process of evolution where something comes out of nothing! Teaching and modelling must go together.

By experience

Often, when a church or group makes the transition to exuberant praise, musicians and worshippers who enjoy this style of music will be attracted to it. This will put pressure on those committed to traditional elements of worship, particularly the choir. Often the choir is the first thing to go, along with the organist. However, the choir can be part of your worship team. Encourage them to be expressive, radiating the love of Jesus, and they will act as a wonderful model of genuine worship. Help the group to learn the songs so that they do not become dependant upon or restricted by the need for books or overhead projection. Let them keep their own copies of words, music, tapes, to assist them in private devotions. This will also bring a familiarity that will help to facilitate greater freedom.

By enlisting the Holy Spirit

Remember that change takes time. Except in the case of a radical revival, a change in heart attitude doesn't happen to everyone simultaneously. It happens to individuals as they are prayed for, taught, loved and given opportunity to worship.

In Conclusion . . . I am convinced that as the Spirit of God brings times of refreshing to his people, we will no longer have to convince them to sing his praises. It will be all we are able to do to provide them with enough opportunity to praise our wonderful God. However, in the transition process, be patient, kind, gentle, long suffering, show mercy, be gracious and above all, love the people. Endeavour to win their hearts more than the argument. After all, worship is more than a style, so how about also rediscovering some of the great hymns of faith?

There's often a sting in the tail!

5 How to Use
The Resource for Small Group Worship

The Resource for Small Group Worship has been devised with convenience and flexibility in mind. Taking into account also the breadth of worship experience and expression, this resource seeks to provide creative opportunities for 'all-age worship' without being either too condescending or too academic.

Convenience For the all-too-busy group leader, this resource provides a complete worship experience that includes:

- Worship songs: gently contemporary, easy to follow without being predictable.

- Meditation: wordless worship, a time to pause, reflect, consider and listen to God.

- Bible readings: arranged for corporate, responsive or personal reading.

- Prayers: written in non-religious language, for corporate or personal use.

- Discussion topics: touching issues of faith, essentials of life, challenges in society.

- Creative activities: always fun, never too exclusive, certain to build group relationships.

Each worship session comes in two parts:

1 The Notes for Leader preparation section, which comprises:

- an introduction to the theme
- a list of resources required
- notes for leading the session, with extracts from relevant books and materials for further activities.

2 Worship Session material. The following icons are used to identify section of the worship material or format. *Only pages with a large underlying icon may be photo-copied, or pages of artwork to be used by the group*:

Ⓞ Opening words (including worship song)

Ⓜ Meditation and listening to God

Ⓡ Reading from the Bible

Ⓟ Prayer and praise (including worship songs)

Ⓕ Further activities, discussion, study and creative ideas

Ⓒ Closing words

A full programme would take about 1 hour to complete.

Variety In order to provide as wide a range material as possible, each volume of *The Resource for Small Group Worship* contains:

- three sessions of general worship
- one session aimed at families and children
- one session which focuses on social awareness and specific issues.

Flexibility *The Resource for Small Group Worship* can be used more selectively by leaders looking for:

- song selection
- meditation ideas
- thematic material
- specialist topics – e.g. social awareness, church festivals, seasonal issues, special occasions
- group activities – drama, craft-work and suchlike
- written prayers.

Though much of the groundwork has been done here for the group leader, the role of that leader is still crucial. Enlist the help of the Holy Spirit at all times so that the worship is truly 'in Spirit and truth'. Lead the people into an experience that more than fills a programme but also affects their homes, marriages, relationships, attitudes, and jobs: their whole lives.

May this resource be a blessing to you, your groups and churches.

Chris Bowater

Conclusion

The Resource for Small Group Worship has been devised and developed in response to a growing desire within churches to be more creative in their worship. For some, there is a wish to bring more creativity into whole church meetings. For others, the development of cells as a model of church life has raised fundamental questions about what it means to worship God in a small-group environment.

The Resource for Small Group Worship does not seek to engage in an in-depth theological discussion on this question, but rather to provide practical starting points for those wishing to explore ways of being creative in worship. The resources are neither exhaustive or prescriptive. They can be used in a variety of ways, providing a springboard for exploration and experimentation.

Hopefully, some of the suggestions will spark off other creative thoughts and ideas. Many can be developed much further than space here permits. Some ideas will work better in the home-group environment, others can be easily adapted to a wider church meeting. The ideas are designed to be as relevant to children and young people as they are to adults.

For some, many of the concepts here will not be new; for others they will present a real challenge, but with a willingness to experiment and learn, they should provide opportunities for people to grow together as they discover new aspects of the infinitely creative God we worship.